UNDER MY WINDOW

George W. Gould

Under My Window
Copyright © 2025 George W. Gould

Produced and printed by Stillwater River Publications. All rights reserved. Written and produced in the United States of America. This book may not be reproduced or sold in any form without the expressed, written permission of the author and publisher.

Visit our website at **www.StillwaterPress.com** for more information.

First Stillwater River Publications Edition.

ISBN: 978-1-965733-29-5

1 2 3 4 5 6 7 8 9 10
Written by George W. Gould.
Cover & interior book design by Matthew St. Jean.
Cover illustration by Christine E. Guadagnino.
Interior illustrations by George W. Gould.
Published by Stillwater River Publications,
West Warwick, RI, USA.

Publisher's Cataloging-in-Publication
(Provided by Cassidy Cataloguing Services, Inc.)
Names: Gould, George W., 1947- author.
Title: Under my window / George W. Gould.
Description: First Stillwater River Publications edition. | West Warwick, RI, USA : Stillwater River Publications, [2025]
Identifiers: ISBN: 978-1-965733-29-5
Subjects: LCSH: Animals--Poetry. | Bird watching--Poetry. | Families--Poetry. | Life--Poetry. | Santa Claus (Fictitious character)--Poetry. | LCGFT: Poetry. | Christmas poetry.
Classification: LCC: PS3607.O88456 U54 2025 | DDC: 811/.6--dc23

The views and opinions expressed in this book are solely those of the author and do not necessarily reflect the views and opinions of the publisher.

*To Sarah and George: Making and inspiring
their own greatest and joyful prosody.*

Contents

Preface .... *vii*

Section 1: Camperberry Tails
Under My Window 1
The Horse's Tail 5
The Squirrel's Tail 11
The Fox's Tail 13
A Lot of Bull 14
Andy the Aardvark 18
The Skunks' Tails 21
The Tail 24
The Weasel's Tail 30
The Missing Tail 33
The Mouse's Tail 35
The Rabbit's Tail (A sonnet) 37
At the End of the Storm 38

Section 2: The Bird Band
SHSHSHHH! 41
Bright Yellow Sunshine 43
Dunlin Fun 45
It Happens at Midnight 50
New England Intruder 53

Section 3: Family Tales
Grampy's Sarah 57
Ballerina Kate 59

Applesauce 60
At Aunt Wheezy's 63
The Last Movie 65
(The After Night) 67
The Night Ride 69
Ode to Aging Poet 71
Zana's Lullaby 72
After Graduation 74

Section 4: People, Places, and Plausibilities
The Piano Man 77
Just Plain Jane 80
Unwrap 81
Names 83
Fenway Forever 85
The Incisor Man, or Dr. Annicelle Is In 87
Today's Poem 89
Timeless 90
Melody in Harmony for the Sake of Melody 91
The Dream 92

Section 5: Santa's
A Christmas Story 95
Santa's More Than Christmas 100
Santa Lives 101

Acknowledgments 103
About the Author 104

PREFACE

To begin with, it is almost always my hope that readers enjoy these poems by reading them aloud.

I have organized my first book in five sections. Plus, there are some poems that are accompanied by photographs, originally in color, or color sketches I have drawn, that appear in black and white. The first sketch, a noisy grackle, announces the book's beginning. The last sketch, a bright red cardinal, symbolizes finishing this book and foreshadows the wings for the books to come.

Section 1: *The Camperberry Tails:* Originally, this section was designed to be its own book, relating stories about animals and borrowing the main plot line format from The Canterbury Tales. The animals build their own church. Then, the first poem of this section establishes a community of animals telling stories about themselves and/or each other. Eventually I plan to expand this section into my next book.

Section 2: *The Bird Band:* In college I became involved with an unauthorized student publication called "The Free Being." The Editor introduced me to the beauty and joys of Birding. He went on to teach in Vermont and unfortunately I lost track of him. In a busy world I lost track of birding too for several years. But, I will never forget the first time he showed me a Rose Breasted Grosbeak with its bright red breast and amazing wobbling song. Thankfully, my wife and I found birding again many years later. Birds are an amazing part of this Earth that is well worth saving.

Our planet and the life forms upon it are in danger. Some scientists think we are already too late to save it. What has to be unequivocally obvious is that to do nothing or even less than everything possible, can only ensure the dire future predictions.

The animals are already victims. They have no ability to change the environment, but they do warn us of our planet's harmful turns by the changes to their health. Animal life is likely our canary in the coal mine. Based on the things happening around us today: higher ocean water temperatures, more catastrophic rain events, larger more powerful storms and horrific fires, ice caps melting, the massive losses of birds every recent migration; we can't afford to have anyone on the sidelines or actively working to keep the status quo when the stakes are so high.

Section 3: *Family Tales,* The poems in this section are composed from family experiences. Occasionally, I have writer's block for fairly long periods of time. Writing poems about my family often helps to get me through those bouts.

However, one such family inspired poem does not appear in this book though. The poem, inspired by the incident below, just did not seem to fit into this book's friendly format.

Every parent has to face taking their child to get a shot or blood work. My two year old needed to get a blood test from the local hospital. I was determined to help her get through it without being frightened by the dreaded needles.

She was crying as we started down the hospital corridor

with her face buried into my shoulder. I stopped, bent down, set her feet on the floor and tried to comfort her. After a minute or so I was just looking for a distraction. I asked her if she'd ever seen a Snizzlerat? She took a baby's breath in through her nose to steady herself, "No Daddy," she sniffed, "What's that?"

Not knowing where I was going with this, I said, "I really don't know. I hoped you'd seen one. People have told me a Snizzlerat is fuzzy and cute— and they live in hospitals to cheer up little children."

My daughter stopped crying.

"But," I continued, "They are really hard to find. They can be almost anywhere?"

Down the hall, we snuck up to the cross corridors and peeked around each corner. We looked under two wheelchairs parked against the wall. When a nice lady told my daughter she was pretty, my daughter told her we were looking for a Snizzlerat.

When we explained what a Snizzlerat was, The lady opened up her knitting bag and said, "I might have seen a glimpse of one in my knitting." But we didn't see one there. When we got into the reception area, the receptionist moved out of the way so my daughter could look under her desk. Still, no Snizzlerat.

The nurse called us into the lab and my daughter started to cry again. As the nurse finished preparing the syringe, I said, "I think a Snizzlerat would say, bimble-boozle-toozle. She stopped crying, her teardrop filled eyes looked up at me with a slight twinkle.

She said something like, "No, they say, foodie, gooses, poopy." She giggled as the nurse swabbed her arm.

I said, "What about, fiddle, caddie, peeple piddle?"

"Just a little pinch," said the nurse. "Almost finished."

My daughter barely noticed. She started to say another slew of silly words when the Nurse said, "All done."

Of course I said, "See it wasn't all that bad."

My daughter looked at me like, 'Didn't I see what she just went through?' but then she smiled.

"Can we go now Daddy?" And she grabbed my hand. We left the lab quickly.

As we walked back down the corridor, my daughter was still looking for a Snizzlerat. We got to the exit door. While I opened the door, my daughter turned around for one last look.

"Look Daddy! I see a Snizzlerat!!!"

I turned around and there was nothing there. But to this day, my daughter swears a fuzzy and cute little creature ran across the corridor down where the two corridors intersect.

There is a Snizzlerat poem in the Santa's section of this book. The original Snizzlerat poem was not about the incident that inspired this story, and did not seem to fit into the book format. That poem will be in my next book. Not putting the original poem in this one leaves more books and poems to do as life continues.

My father-in-law, a designer by trade and an artist by avocation, always left a small place in each painting unfinished, almost always it was hard to find. He always said that nothing is ever really finished and all life needs a little mystery leftover. If you can't wait until the next book, go to my website and see if you can find the button that opens up to The Snizzlerat poem. It probably won't be that hard to find; but if you can't find it there (and it will be there), you can send me an email and I'll email you a copy.

The Family section of poems is inspired by a family member or based on a family incident. Growing up I was mostly in awe of my family. My little section of poems is in no way representative of all the wonderful family poems to come in future writings.

Section 4, *People, Places and Plausibility:* This is a collection of eclectic poems. Some of the poems were inspired by an event or several events, perhaps a life experience.

These are poems that were interesting and wanted to be written.

Section 5: *Santa's:* For a while now, I have been writing Christmas Santa Claus poems every year. Santa Claus has evolved significantly through the ages in good times and bad. Santa has always been able to change to meet the times, maybe better than any other religious figure. Regardless of his physical appearance including gender, his character and philosophical purpose is to help all children become adults.

Discovering poetry and, better than that, actually writing poetry is another wonderful experiment and experience in my life. I have learned a lot about poetry. I tried to write several forms of poems and some of those attempts are a part of this book. Whether they are good enough for purists doesn't really matter, does it? I had a wonderful time writing them. I will continue to compose and write poems for the rest of my life and I hope you, the reader, will enjoy this book just for the joy of it.

Section 1

Camperberry Tails

Under My Window

The Downy Woodpecker
And all of his kin
Announced renovation
About to begin.

So under my window
On papery birch
Testily tapping
They started a church.

They built from the roots
Of the birch that survive
A silvery house
Looking truly alive.

That brought out the ravens
The squirrels and a crow
Adding tinsel and tin
That reflected a glow.

The wind winding tinsel
Mirrored the sun,
While the tingling tin
Tuned the wind too for fun.

The rustling leaves
Wove a yellow and brown
Spiraling steeple
Seen all over town.

That brought in some bats
To live in the belfry,
And brought in poor mice
To pray for the wealthy.

That brought in the moles
And the skunks and the dogs.
The pews weren't reserved;
They just pulled up some logs.

They gathered the badger
A chipmunk or two,
Raccoons and possums,
And a goat trip trapped through.

A very large horse
Who lived in the barn
Stepped to the pulpit
To spin us his yarn.

But before he could start
A goose flew on in
A duck quacked his way
Through the crowd and the din.

A pig pushed on through
And a cat purred to play
A sparrow perched near
And decided to stay.

And a little pink nose
That twitched as a habit
Jumped out from the rose
Attached to a rabbit.

They all had a story
They wanted to tell;
They all were crusaders
All different as well.

For one afternoon
They huddled together.
They just beat the rain
And some very foul weather.

Regardless of credo,
Appearance, belief;
In this little church
They could all find relief.

It wasn't a church
That required the same;
It wasn't a church that
Made you feel shame.

In this little church
They all had decided
To celebrate difference,
And with love to be guided;

And then the big horse
Reaching 20 hands tall
Neighed for attention
And silenced them all.

And the stories began:

The Horse's Tail
(Filly's Flight For the Roses)

Regret
Is the horse
Of renowned;
And today
She will run
With the wind
When the race
Will begin.
    And the beat, And the beat,
        Of her heart and her feet,
            Will decide how her journey will end.

Note to reader:
Regret was the first filly to win the Kentucky Derby.

It's the first
Of the day
And the skies
Rising high,
And she knows
She'll endure;
But her trainer's unsure.
She is different somehow
And she just won't allow,
Someone to get in her way!
It's her day!
And the beat, And the beat,
    Of her heart and her feet,
        Will decide how her journey will end.
But for now
Calming down,
As she hears from the past,
Beating hooves
Beating back
All the time
Running hard
And she thinks
To herself
"We stand tall.
We stand tall."
And she knows
How she stands for us all.
And the beat, And the beat,
    Of her heart and her feet,
        Will decide how her journey will end.

By a stir
In her stall
Darting eyes
Growing tall,
Jockeys Up.
And Her heart
Skips a beat
When they trumpet
The call.
    And the beat, And the beat,
        Of her heart and her feet,
            Will decide how her journey will end.
On the track
Her head shakes
And she snorts
As she turns
In a loop.
Then she slips,
Starts to fall,
But she's quick
To pick up;
And she loads
In the gate.
Then she waits
For the bell;
They release
Her front wall!
    And the beat, And the beat,
        Of her heart and her feet.
            Will decide how her journey will end.

She sprints
To the front
With affront
To the males:
They're bigger,
And stronger.
She runs
With such gall.
She is two
Lengths ahead.
And she's all
By herself.
As she runs
With the wind
It's her day
After all.
    And the beat, And the beat,
        Of her heart and her feet,
            Will decide how her journey will end.
Not second
But first,
And it must
Be a dream;
And her heart
Runs ahead
Singing out
Its proud call;
And her heart
Runs ahead.

Running fast!
    And the beat, And the beat,
        Of her heart and her feet,
            And she ran, and she ran,
                And she ran— the fastest of all!!
And the beat, and the beat, and the beat,
    and the beat, echoes on.

The Squirrel's Tail
(Nuts to You)

Squirrels scooted and looted
The nuts from the trees,
And danced through the branches
And scattered the leaves.

Skittered and scampered
And scratched up a tree,
Hung upside down
Eating birdseed with glee.

Squirrel proofing measures
On feeders don't work;
The squirrel only looks
At those things with a smirk.

Hanging ones, clanging ones,
The stands that are crook'd,
They're not even defeated
By the ones that are gooked.

They run on the lawns,
And riff through the flowers,
Eating my pears
And my apples for hours.

There's nothing that scares them,
No bang, no big rock,
No rattle, or roller
Or smelly gym sock.

I tried out the latter
In sad desperation;
They stuffed it with nuts
For the long hibernation.

By the way I can tell you,
Hibernation's a myth;
They tore up my attic
Last December the fifth.

There's nothing quite like though
The way that they play;
They entertain me for peanuts
So I hope they will stay.

The Fox's Tail
(The Loop)   *Villanelle*

The Farmer locked the chicken coop
And thought he took away the key;
The fox was never in the loop.

The chickens cheeped themselves to sleep
And thought the lock would keep them free;
The Farmer locked the chicken coop.

Each day the lock he thought would keep
The chickens safe and free to be.
The fox was never in the loop.

The fox went by to take a peek;
He gave the lock the third degree.
The Farmer locked the chicken coop.

By now a plan began to creep.
Into the fox, as you can see,
The fox was never in the loop.

The farmer paid a price quite steep.
A chicken meal was fox's fee.
The Farmer locked the chicken coop.
The fox was never in the loop.

The Moose's Tail
(A Lot of Bull)

The crotchety old man
Fried potatoes in his pan
As he listened to
The eager little boy.

The boy is frowning as he spoke
As his eyes fill up with smoke.
"You say you've often seen a moose?
And they're out there on the loose?"

"Ayuh," he says and spits,
And the fire sizzled fits.
"I see 'em almost every day.
On the trail they're in the way."

"Well," said the boy,

"I looked over by the bees.
I thought I saw some boney knees.
In the crispy autumn breeze,
It was just some knotty trees.

On a Mount Katahdin hike
That the black flies seemed to like,
Not a moose, no hide, no hair
But I did attract a bear.

At Freeport's L.L. Bean,
A bull moose had just been seen.
Of course, the one I saw that day
Was in a window on display.

In Skowhegan it was cold.
23 below I'm told.
There were moose tracks on the ground;
But not a moose was ever found.

Up in Aroostook County,
They offered up a bounty.
We looked all day and night,
Not a moose came into sight."

"That's ah-nuff," the old man spoke,
Gave his cheek a little poke
With his tongue, and a laugh
He told the boy he'd made a gaffe.

"Yah cahnt nevah see a moose,
One 'specially on the loose.
A moose will always stay at bay
Until yah look the other way.

My advice tah you tahday,
Take a rest or go and play.
Moose'll make yah go insane
If yah choose ta' stay in Maine."

So his mom took him away
And the boy was heard to say,
"There's no moose on the loose."
As they walked past the caboose,

Then they climbed up on the train
To leave the State o' Maine.
The train began to lurch,
But then it stopped beside a church.

(Woooo-oo-woo. Woooo-oo-woo.)

The whistle in the train
Began to blow a shrill refrain.
Soon the train was so delayed
That the sun began to fade.

But, the train just sat there still
Until the boy had had his fill,
And decided to declare
He'd sooner walk to Delaware

Than to sit a second more
Behind the train's big wooden door.
So, he jumped down off the back
And made a beeline up the track.

It seemed he walked a mile or two
Before the Engine came in view.
"Stop!" cried the Engineer.
But the boy just wouldn't hear.

As they chased him down the track,
The boy just laughed as he looked back.
And when he turned his head around
Something knocked him to the ground.

When they finally brought him to,
A dozen people came in view.
Excitement filled their eyes
As they asked to his surprise,

"Did yah see the big Bull Moose?"
"The one that's out there on the loose?"
"The one that blocked the railroad track?"
"The one that knocked you on your back?"

Almost everyone that day
Had seen the moose just walk away,
And the one who ran into it?
Wasn't lookin' when he viewed it.

Andy the Aardvark
a good night story

He peeked in his room...then turned on the light...
He pulled down the shades to keep out the night.

He sniffed at the air and snuffed with his snout,
Then crept into bed after checking it out.

This nocturnal animal is called an aardvark,
But Andy the Aardvark's afraid of the dark.

His mommy and daddy were very concerned;
Living at night it had to be learned;

That's when you eat, when the food's fast asleep,
Not in the day when your food runs away.

His Mommy kept saying, "It's all up to you.
You are the one to decide what to do."

And Daddy had told him, "The dark is your friend.
It helps you get food, keeps you safe in the end."

A light in the hall, they tried that at first;
But monstery shadows made that dark the worst.

They tried a night-light to get over his fear;
But he worried all night that the dark would appear.

When he closed his eyes, they asked, "What do you see?"
He screamed, "Not a thing! It's just too dark for me!"

But then came the night when the lights all went out,
Batteries died, their replacements in doubt.

Mommy and Daddy were gathering food;
And, they weren't around when their Aardvark unglued.

Into the night, he went searching for light,
Exhausting himself and shaking with fright.

Crawling around, he bumped into a mound;
And inside the mound, some termites were found.

Now termites to you might not be to eat;
But termites to Aardvarks are a fabulous treat.

He unrolled his tongue which was sticky with goo,
And licked up this food without stopping to chew.

Andy kept thinking, Mom and Dad might be right;
So he made up his mind to end fear on this night.

He finished his termites, looked up at the sky.
He took a deep breath and he gave a big sigh.

As stars had come out and they dotted above;
The light from those stars made his fear turn to love.

Andy the Aardvark thought dark isn't bad;
And the night-lights above from the stars that he had

Made dark in the night like a blanket to warm us
And the brave that he felt grew up to enormous.

Now Andy decided to help mom and dad.
He gathered up termites, the rest that he had.

He brought them all home in the dark of the night.
His mom and his dad rejoiced at the sight.

As daylight arrived, they all went to bed
To celebrate Andy and darkness instead.

The Skunks' Tails
(There's a Skunk Under the Porch!)

What can we do?
Just leave him alone.
But he's under the porch!
Well then, throw him a bone.

Skunks don't eat bones.
They eat mostly grubs,
Those fat little worms
That eat bulbs down to nubs.

If Skunks don't eat grubs
The flowers won't grow;
Their rainbow of colors
Our children won't know.

Maybe the dog could chase him away?
He's under the bed, shaking with fear.
He's had a skunk shower.
Remember last year?

For crying out loud
A skunk's got to live,
But that odor he leaves
It's so hard to forgive.

He's down in the cellar!

I see him down there!
A cute little feller,
A white stripe in his hair.

He's down in the cellar!
Now what do we do?
Oh no! Look at that!
I think there are two.

Skunks in the cellar
Get rid of those pests!
Call Animal Control
For our unwelcome guests.

They said they're not coming?
It's not really their job?
They suggested we contact
'Ole Pest Control Bob!?

Bob won't come either
Unless we can pay
An outrageous sum
And we pay him today!

At first we resisted,
But the smell, it got worse.
If we waited much longer
They'd be calling a hearse.

Bob came right over;
Collected his dough,
Played a flute and he danced,
But the skunks didn't go?

He pounded a drum,
And he bowed on a fiddle.
He suddenly said,
He could solve a skunk riddle.

Then he said to the skunks:

"Promise to leave.
I'll tell you the tale
How a skunk got its stripe
And why it's so pale."

The skunks whirled around
Coming out of their funk.
What surprised them the most
Was that Bob spoke in skunk.

The skunks nodded agreement
To Bob's little pact;
They both had been wondering
As a matter of fact.

Thankfully, Bob got right to it:

The Skunk's Tail

(How Skunks Got Their Tail (according to Bob))

It was a gray morning;
The witch arose late.
The clouds flew by swiftly—
A loud crash at the gate.

The witch went with haste
To check out the fuss,
She was instantly smitten
By this sweet little cuss.

A black little kitten
From his head to his toe
With a wide swishy tail
On his neck was a bow.

On the bow it was written
What the witch thought was code,
Sounding creepy and scary
Like the song from a toad.

"Noom-revo-moorb
A-raos-erom-reven"
Could never be terms
That came down from heaven.

She spoke these words slowly
She spoke them three times
A light flashed in the distance
She thought she heard chimes.

The cat was a beauty
With his black shiny coat
Was purr-fectly pleasing
Amusingly remote.

There was a small drawback
She smelled right away.
This cat had an odor
That grew harsher each day.

Since a witch isn't known
For her number of friends;
A harsh smell to us
A witch always defends.

But the witch's worst nightmare
Had also occurred.
Her magic was gone.
Her psyche was blurred.

She couldn't scare children
Or make magic potions
Nor ride on her broom
Or put lizards in lotions.

She tried to get help
But she had no success;
And only her cat
Was there to caress.

She carried her cat
Wherever she went,
And clothes pinned her nose
From the unpleasant scent.

As she passed by the mirror
One particular day,
It was more than just shocking.
She was speechless they say.

As she looked in the mirror
On the back of the door
The words on the bow
Weren't in code anymore.

They were regular words
From some snake in the grass.
The words on the bow
Were reversed in the glass.

"This must be from Harold,"
She thought to herself,
"That rascally trickster
Who's one-quarter elf."

"Never-more-soar
A-broom-over-moon"
His spell took her magic
That mean old buffoon.

She thought of the day
She heard chimes and saw light.
She'd first lost her magic
That very same night.

She loved her black cat
Who's a little remote.
And she loved to caress
His black shiny coat.

She loved his big eyes;
And his wide swishy tail
And the way he curled up
At her feet without fail.

But without her black magic
It wasn't the same;
And she knew that the cat
Was the cause and to blame.

With a lot of regret
She turned the cat out,
And made some slight changes
To help all witches out.

A white stripe on his back
That's easily seen;
It wasn't a red,
Or an orange or green.

It was a pale white
To be seen just at night
By the ghouls and the goblins
That stayed out of the light.

And a witch in the sky
Who was flying around
Would not think this cat
Was just lost on the ground;

Would not take it home
And lose all of their magic,
Because as you've seen
Losing magic is tragic.

Bob finished by saying,
"When you see a wild skunk
It's only a cat,
With a white stripe, that stunk."

His story now ended
And the skunks were offended.
To say they were cats
Just must be rescinded.

Living under the porch
Would no longer do.
A Skunk never stays
Where there's held such a view.

The Skunks moved next door
To Rhoda's old shed;
But they still ate our grubs
Saving all flowerbeds.

Our children have learned
About rainbows and flowers
And sing songs about Spring
And gentle rain showers.

Today there's no Skunks
Who live under our porch;
And I'm sure you're aware
We don't carry a torch.

We know they aren't cats.
But please, don't ever tell them.
We like having flowers
And now we can smell them.

The Weasel's Tail

At first they were glad
Sitting under our birch
In harmony's light
From building the church.

Then smoke from our fire
Became thicker than fog,
And stench filled each nose
As they sat on their log.

The smoke cleared away
But the odor still stayed
And out of the smoke
A weasel waylaid.

He tiptoed as softly
As cotton on skin
And flashed deadly eyes
And a sinister grin.

He whispered his tale
Through razor sharp teeth
And hissed as he spoke
His foreshadowed bequeath

"I love to just slink
And slip through the night
Cause death and destruction
With one well placed bite.

Don't count all your chicks
Or leave ducks unattended,
I can't help myself and
Their lives will be ended.

I'm thirsty for blood
That is fresh from the kill.
I get great satisfaction
And killing's a thrill.

Not fricasseed, boiled,
Or barbecued fest,
Just raw to the bone
Is always the best.

To all who are careless
Or conceited enough
To believe they are safe
From this rough kind of stuff,

Whatever you do,
Do not take my dares,
Be wary of me
I'm the worst of nightmares.

A weasel's a bogeyman,
One of those thugs,
A shark in the water,
A seller of drugs.

Your life is too precious;
My tale is your clue.
This is my last warning.
My next target's **YOU!!**

The weasel was gone
Just as quick as he came
As he went back to prey
On the weak and the lame.

The Missing Tail
(A History of the Dodo)

Then, a sad looking bird stepped slowly forward,
Outlined in the smoke and the fire,
Dressed like a gray paper-doll, but certain pieces missing.

It spoke, saying:
"I once knew an odd ole bird.
He had, a round abounding abdomen
An angly, dangly tail.
A bulbous, pachydermic bill.
A woolly warble in his whistle.
A crinkled expression with his smile.
He came to me all dressed in gray.
A Charlie Chaplin gait.
The Portuguese came, and laughed out loud,
And rolling tears came down their cheeks.
The crazy, foolish 'Doudo' bird
Became the sailors' food.
Then rats and pigs from ships
Came too, and ate the giant eggs.
One hundred years went by.
And even taxidermy disappeared in 1755.
Extinction came for 400 years.
But tomorrow,

A chance I may become again."
Three letters formed in the smoke:
D N A
Then Dodo bird, a flightless bird,
Arose into the smoke,
His crinkled smile continued clinging
In the darkness.

The Mouse's Tail

Creeping—tippy toes, tingle in the snow.
Slippery—twitchery, musn't go too slow.
Mind the shadows from above,
Hiding in a girl's lost glove,
Waiting for the sun to go,
Lying still and laying low.

Weepy—wispy eyes, looking for her glove
Knittery—jittery, grandma's made with love.
Tracing steps she made before,
Walking through the barn back door.
Giving it a little shove,
Startling a mourning dove.

Out pops the nose and little more.
The whiskers wonder what's in store.
Coming next are big brown eyes,
Widening in big surprise!

The little girl lifts up her glove.
The little mouse looks up above.
They smile and blink and tremble too;
They do not know quite what to do.

The mouse jumps down and runs away.
The happy girl goes on her way.
Her glove is warm all through and through;
The mouse escapes to start anew.

The Rabbit's Tail (A sonnet)
(The Heart's Song of Life)

A rose has pricked the subtle satin night
And brought the dawn with lucid pearly dew;
And stretched the flower buds as breezes blew.
Then sleepy sounds of June bugs waved in light.
The wait has opened up the meadow's sight.
The moon's eye watches wistfully the view.
And sweet Bermuda's green just bends anew
In syncopated rhythms dark and bright.
In time, I move beyond my safest place
I nibble first upon the sparsest grass;
My wrinkled nose precedes my giggle's charm.
I then evade the spider's webs of lace.
To taste the luscious blades I stayed the pass,
And wiggle through myself without alarm.

At the End of the Storm

At the end of the storm
The sun took a chance
Do-si-doed with the clouds
Flying by in their dance.

The gathering knew,
As they slowly disbanded,
Their lives would return
To what life had demanded.

But not the distrusting
What someone believes,
Or being a bully,
Or living as thieves.

But learning to recognize
Imperfect glitches;
And how to exist
In their own little niches.

They felt quite uplifted
Leaving after it rained;
And gladdened in heart
From the knowledge they'd gained.

Section 2

The Bird Band

SHSHSHHH!

Henrietta heron stands stately, staring;
A statue stealthily standing still,
Neither a shiver,
Nor a quiver, as she stood.
She was preying, her quarry praying,
Hoping the preyer never knew.
Patience preying. Skittish praying.
Deadly danger studies stutters, flutters,
Front leg folded, balanced.
Striking lightning.
Deadly dangles, shaking, shaken, shook
Swallowed whole.
Standing still again.

Bright Yellow Sunshine

Magnolia trees came out today
With blossoms pink to greet the sun,
And George was out today to play;
He chased a squirrel that tried to run
Away, and scamper up the tree;
Then stopped to chatter angrily!

George's interest had moved on.
A yellow flitter that was tossed
By gusts of wind, now here and gone
Across the tree, then perched aloft.

At first he thought it was a leaf,
But something strange changed his belief.
Supposedly a leaf can't sing
Or fly itself against the wind;
But this leaf sang and flew a ring
Alighting on his shoulder, like a friend.

George was pleasantly surprised
And stayed as quiet as he could
Just as Grampy had advised.
So his new friend, the tiny bird
Of yellow, green and black and white,
Sang his song of weeta-weeta-weeteo;
Then flew back to the tree just out of sight;
And George went running happily to let his Grampy know.

Note to reader:
It's fun to watch a bird take flight,
Fly toward the sun and out of sight;
But when a bird sits on its nest,
We need to do our very best
To help our feathered friend stay safe,
And not disturb their nesting place.

Dunlin Fun

While making mud pies with his hands
And building castles in the sands,

George looked up upon the rocks
And Dunlins rested there in flocks.

Dunlins stared with one dark eye;
And George decided he knew why.
George was thinking he just knew,
That 'Dunlin birds play Peek-a-boo?'

Creeping slowly down the sand;
he crawled along hand over hand;
creeping, creeping, never peeking
not a sound was even peeping.

Feet to go and George got ready,
ready... ready. Steady ready.
Before he took his final chance
George just took another glance...

The Dunlin birds?— had flown away?
But not too far; he still could play.
George bent down, moved closer still;
this time he moved, behind a hill.

From just behind some craggy rocks,
he jumped up like a Jack-in-a-box!

George yelled out, as his size grew,
"Peek-a-boo, 'cause I see you!!"

The startled birds knew they'd been caught.
At least, by George, that's what he thought.
They flew away, into the sun,
And George just smiled—he knew he'd won.

The End

It Happens at Midnight

The Moon out at night on the night before last
Turned night into day 'til the clouds rolled in fast.
From our perch on the porch lit by flickering torch,
The moon flickered too as the clouds flew on through.
A damp clammy mist oozed off of the pond
A lonely loon lingered a cry from beyond.

Hooolii Hooolii

"It's time," said my Uncle; "We can't wait until morning.
It happens at midnight." The loon shrieked a warning.

Hahahahahaha!!

"W-Where are we going?" I looked with askance.
He said, "To the forest to see the night dance."
"There may be a murder." He whispered a "Shushsh."
"You don't need to worry: We're behind a big bushsh."

The clouds move on by and our feet rustle leaves
The ooze makes it foggy. I wish for more breeze.
One stone at a time as mist is subsiding;
A gate to a graveyard, whose graves are residing?

The moss on the gravestones covers the names;
I ponder the dreary, the sadness and shames.
An epitaph reads "**Prepare for the end**"
A chill makes me shiver, what tragedies portend?

We crossover tracks. A train's coming soon.
The clouds slowly pass through the light of the moon.
Two minutes to midnight, we arrive at our spot
I hear gurgles and pops; I smell odor and rot.

And just in that instant the mist dissapates.
The moon reappears to determine our fates.
My uncle's behind me; I don't know what to do.
The shadows are creeping. I hope we'll pass through.

I look up to see, trees filled with black crows.
There must be a thousand, their smell fills my nose.

WOOO—OO—WOOO!!!

The steely train whistle had startled the night
The crows flew around me, obscuring my sight.
They fly toward the darkness, then spiraled around
They look like they're dancing from down on the ground.

My uncle cries, "Murder!!" and loudly proclaims,
"They're coming here next to punish and maim!!
I dove in the bush. But my uncle just crows
While the crows landed softly right back in their rows.

The dancing at midnight was exciting to see
The number of crows was amazing to me.
My uncle explained that a large flock of crows
Is considered "a murder," a fact I should know.

The sky became quiet. Clouds covered the moon.
I made peace with my uncle, and the loon seemed to swoon

Whe—ooo—quee

New England Intruder
(The Black Vulture)

It's a mystery in my history
Why my home is where it is.
My old bones are in Europe,
But it's not the place I live.

Today I live across the sea,
America's where I roam;
And no one here can tell me
Why I left my other home.

I carry on with carrion;
I soar around the sky;
I hang around where humans live,
You think you can guess why?

We follow turkey look-a-likes
'Cause they can smell our foods.
They use their noses to do this.
They think they're clever dudes.

They don't like what happens next,
But in the wild we feel
Their garbage or dead animals
Becomes our next big meal.

Section 3

Family Tales

Grampy's Sarah

She talks to me in yaws and yahs instead of saying yes.
Then twinks her eyes to let me know the rest I have to guess.
I love to guess what's going on or how she played that day;
Sometimes I'm right and she says "yaw," and we begin to play;
But when I'm wrong, or she gets bored, I hear a little moan;
She shakes her head, then turns around, and leaves
    me all alone.

It's great to be a Grampy when Sarah says my name.
She doesn't quite say Grampy or even quite the same.
It seems to be a cross between a bramble and a grumpy;
But when she calls me brampy the thorns just
    aren't so bumpy.
And when she calls me brumpy my edges seem to melt;
The grump that's in my grumpy soothes the way
    I would have felt.

We walked along a foggy pond one soggy afternoon.
We spied a boxy turtle and a froggy jump too soon.
We saw it just an instant, we heard the froggy say,
"Ribbit y Ribbit, Ribbit y Ribbit," before he swam away.
Then Sarah pointed to the place the froggy'd been before
And she began to hop around, then it began to pour.

We both hopped to the shelter, then ran out to the cars;
We watched the crackily zigity zags that zoomed like
    lighted stars.

I told her it was lightning; she told me it was "boom!"
We giggled to see the " boomity-boom" scare away
    the dark and gloom.
After a while the sun came out and shone down through
    the rain,
And then a rainbow out of the blue was all that did remain.

The morning and the afternoon they always go too fast
When Sarah's time with Grampy surely slips into the past,
I'll miss the rain we hopped into when rainbows filled
    our eyes;
But every chance to play again will bring a new surprise.
I hope the day will never come when we will grow too old,
To be surprised by something new that's still our pot of gold.

Ballerina Kate

Oh happy girl, of twirl and whirl
Spinning her merry, and merry go round,
Balanced—then swirled, this girl of a pearl,
Sailing her songs, and softest of curl.

Kate's cheeks of round painted apple-y plum,
The supplely sounds, and the happily hums,
Taffeta pink flows round and around,
Feet fast and frilled skimming over the ground.

Oh happy girl you dance with the clouds
Spinning your spell and winning the crowds,
Dancing away and growing too fast,
Weaving a memory into the past.

Applesauce

Grandma decided to go to the store
And Dad told my mom he was doing a chore.
Then Mom took some time to just run to next door.
My sister spilled applesauce out on the floor.

My sister's Picasso of applesauce doodles
With squiggles and wiggles that look like egg noodles,
With blobs of the sauce she makes oodles of poodles,
With sauce on her nose she makes gooey protrudals.

I told her to stop because Mom says it's rude
For children her age to be playing with food.
She hands me a spoon as if me to include
And frowns a big frown like she thinks I'm a prude.

Because it's a day when there's no one around,
I stirred in some spice that's already been ground.
Some cinnamon red, some nutmeg I found,
And curry that's yellow rates "oooh!" for a sound.

I painted a picture with swirls around stars
With green from some basil I took from some jars.
I drew a red barn, then drew yellow cars.
I splashed a red circle that looked just like Mars.

My applesauce picture had colors galore
And that's when my grandma came in through the door.
Her eyes opened wide when she looked at the floor,
And waggled her finger to not do anymore.

Then twinkle and mischief came into one eye.
The next thing we knew she'd decided to try
Applesauce letters. She got to the Y.
It would have been Z but my father came by.

The room was alive with the colors of goo,
And my sister told Dad, "We just did it for you?"
But Dad stood there stern as he took in the view,
And demanded we clean all that goo that we drew.

My sister was squeezing my dad by the hand
When he did a thing I could not understand.
In applesauce goo that my mother had canned
He started a map of American land.

He started in Maine and down the East Coast;
His Florida keys were some crumbs from some toast.
The Texas panhandle he drew with a boast,
"My applesauce map is the best by the most!!"

Then Utah, and Kansas and Illinois too;
And the whole kitchen floor was a map made of goo.
He'd just about finished the oceans of blue
When my mother appeared, from her look we just knew

That she was upset and might go quite berserk,
But instead she just smiled with a cool kind of smirk;
And she yanked out a brush with a herk and a jerk,
And plied on some goo with some great handiwork.

Then out came her camera, a selfie or two,
We stepped ourselves back, and we took in the view.
My mother with sadness said all that we drew,
"It must be cleaned up before goo turns to glue."

We'd found an adventure, and giggled for days.
We laughed as we cleaned up the mess that we made.
Covered with applesauce toenail to top,
We cleaned up the applesauce, every last drop.

"Remember the time we made applesauce art?"
Is often the way conversations will start.
"Applesauce Memories" are the ones that you keep.
They warm you forever even during your sleep.

At Aunt Wheezy's

A golden glaze settled on a summer's early morning
With June bugs already humming.
Hay fevered, crusty covered eyes
Are wiped with a cool damp terry cloth.

Feet jumped into blue-jean coveralls,
Hands, slide shoulder straps up and over,
Grab the tin pail with a wire handle;
My name painted on its side.

Walking into knee-high grassy and shrub laden knolls.
Patches of sandy soil showing wild blueberry bushes
That grew the best blueberries in the State of Maine,
Making them, most likely, the best blueberries ever on earth.

They grew in bunches, in mixed clusters of white,
    red and ripe blue pearls.
The ripe blue ones thumped in a rat-a-tat
As they cascaded from bush, to hand, to the bottom
    of the pail,
Exceptions came shortcutting to mouth, more and more,
The closer the blue pearls came to the pail's top.

Careful in haste is possible,
but never enough to keep a few sour white or red berries
from sneaking in with the best pearls.

In Aunt Wheezy's kitchen my pail is pared to perfection
and the blue pearls melt into magic pie and blueberry cake
that disappears in smiles and delightful, delectable morsels.
Oh my, I can still taste those days.

The Last Movie

What did she say thirty or forty years ago?
"I guess I can die happy now?"
I can't be exactly sure anymore.

She asked me to choose the row.
The theatre had plastic feeling seats.
There wasn't any stadium seating then.
I remember that.

She was sitting on my left.
On reflection, it was clear;
I must have forgotten—Ladies first.

It would have been a rare mistake.
Deference was something I learned from her.
But if I entered the row first, She may not have noticed.
She commanded, but never demanded.

The movie starred an elderly Katherine Hepburn and
    Henry Fonda.
There were haunting Loon voices.
At this moment I can't remember the name of the movie;
I used to know so well.
I thought of her as so much younger than the stars.

We drove home to my house. Happy.
What did we talk about? I wish I had written it down.
We ate dinner, slept, and they left the next day.

When they got home, she called to let me know of her
 safe arrival.
Maybe it was then she said,
'I guess I can die happy now.'

I worked in a prison that year,
And the Nightwatch Commander called me to his office.
My wife was on the phone.

While she was speaking to me,
I thought about how I resented the telephone.
'Why do I have to hear this?' repeated
In my mind until the call ended.

Weeks later at the funeral,
I realized the last words she heard from me were over
 the phone.
"Good-bye Mom. I love you."

And she said, "Good-bye, I love you too."

(The After Night)

You must have been the one
To teach me how to make my eyes smile,
And in all probability to speak in your convincing cadences.

I see soft somnolent eyes and lines and brows,
Weathered in waves, wrinkling with time,
Sparkling through cloudy colored iris blue,
Once sharpened by impish wit
And wide with wonderment.

You must have taught me to tie down the bones,
Then tickle the terms, and stretch to catch
The effervescence of an image.

You were the one that first read to me
The tintinnabulation of Poe
The accent of R-Robert Bur-rns
The fog of Sandburg;

Spellbound me, to The Adventures of Robin Hood
And the "slithy toves" of Alice's Wonderland.

We cried together those nights
Of JFK, RFK and Martin Luther King.
We watched many dawns' early lights
That magnified through the silver surf of Wallis Sands.

Many times you sang soothing songs,
And I clung to you to chase away the monsters of my fears.

The songs today are not quite the same;
Today I can only reminisce our memories, without you.
The features of your face are burned into my memories
   in the mirror, but are almost faceless,
Without you here.

The Night Ride

One night, when fingers of frost
Curled themselves on window panes,
And the full moon's light skimmed down the hill
In straight paths in my backyard, and across the new
Icy crystals left from winter's sun,

I stole softly to my closet and as quickly
As I could, zip up my snowsuit,
Lace my snow boots, sneak
Down the stairs and creep open
The door without it squeaking.

I made my way to the Flexible Flyer
With the smooth red runners and the
Frozen tow rope I ripped from the
Top crusty-hard snow layer,
Causing chunks to glide away like pieces in a wind chime.

I scrambled to the top of the hill,
Saw the man in the moon
Smile his wintery smile,
Then turned,

Holding fast to the straight wooden edges
And facing the front of my Flyer
Down the hill,
I ran and dove onto the back of my sled.

The solitary night, the glistening snow,
Flashed by me
And sparkles of snow flew up from behind
In a crystal comet tail.

Snow and icy crystals sprayed my face
And tongue and melted to my cheeks
All the way down, listening
To the soosh of the runners
And the quiet of the night.

At the bottom, my flyer and I
Glided to a gentle stop.
And I rolled over onto the snow
Watching my breath's vapor
Billow into darkness and the shimmering stars.

Sometime later, I slid myself into bed,
Cocooned into my warm blankets,
And I slept in my smile.

Ode to Aging Poet

The well looks dry— I've lost my muse.
I've got to light another fuse.
At years beyond my middle age,
It is my time to be the Sage.

But,

The Subway bus won't take my token;
The Fork in the Road seems bent and broken.
My mind is muddled with forget-me-knots;
Their fragrance confuses my aging thoughts.

Each hour-glass wrinkle, each hair turning grey,
Adds a layer of panic that won't go away.
My next great thought is likely my best.
I hope it will come before final rest.

Zana's Lullaby

     C   Em
The wind in the meadow
      F   Em
Sings a soft lullaby
    F   Em
The baby boy listens
     Dm   C
And hushes his cry

     C   Em
The morning sunshine
    F   Em
Is warming the day
   F   Em
And soon baby's sleeping
    Dm   G
And dreaming away

    A   G
The world that surrounds you
   F   Em
Is peaceful and calm
     F   Em
You're wrapped in the love
   Dm   G
Of your mother's arms

    C   Em
So sleep little wonder
      F   Em
Your mommy is here
     F   Em
She'll stay by your side
        Dm   C
So there's nothing to fear

     F   Em
She'll stay by your side
        Bm   C
So there's nothing to fear

After Graduation

I hope you never catch your shadow;
May it grow beyond your dreams.
Fill your life with life itself;
And make each step
A measured stride
Igniting stars across the sky.

Section 4

People, Places, and Plausibilities

The Piano Man
(Inspired by David Madara)

To learn piano can be tricky;
A teacher is quite often picky.
You practice playing every day
When all your friends go out to play.

I know it's better for my heart
If I go play without Mozart.
It can't be healthy sitting there
Just wearing holes in underwear.

And then one day I met a man,
Who had a somewhat different plan.
He played for me a quick etude,
And not to listen seemed too rude.

He played it quick and stepped aside
And said this "'tude" would help decide
If I would ever really play
Piano in a "grownup" way.

I thought this 'tude would be my chance
In my mind I did a dance.
If I just played this 'tude real bad
He'd say piano's just a fad.

I stretched my fingers, then sat down,
I gave the man a little frown
As though I'd really try so hard,
Yet in my mind — I'm in the yard:
Playing baseball.

"Excuse me!" said Piano Man,

"Although you missed most all the notes,
I like the way your music floats;
Your fingers flew, the keys just dance.
I think you need another chance."

He made me play etude again
And then I played it once again
I played it worse each time I played
And he gave me a higher grade!?

I played etude one hundred times;
The Great Chopin would call them crimes.
Around ten thousand I confused
The etude notes I had abused.

The mixed up notes had found a way
To play themselves just right that day.
This teacher said, "It was quite stirring;
The notes you played were all alluring."

Ten times that day I played it right
Despite how hard I tried to fight.
"Astounding how you played those keys,
Here's more pieces, please play these."

He gave me several more to play.
I told him, "Please! Just go away."

Then,
I played them all without much stress
It was, like fun I must confess.
That made me want to play some more;
Some more became some twenty-four.

Piano-man? His work was done.
I learned to play. He made it fun.
Another kid had caught his eye;
He tipped his hat and said, "Goodbye."

Just Plain Jane

"Twinkle Twinkle" soft and clear
A little girl was drawing near.
I smiled and hummed about a bar
And sang, " I wonder what you are ?"
She stopped and said, "My name is Jane;"
And then she added, "Just plain, Jane."

I told her that she isn't plain
Though lots of people share her name.
And then I asked if she might know
The other verses; she said, "No."
We talked awhile and did our best
And pretty soon she learned the rest.

As we departed I surmised
That she was really quite surprised
To find a lady with her name,
Jane Taylor was the one who came
To write the words that we all sing.

Since eighteen six her poem brings
Her little star to light the way
For little children every day.
And just because plain rhymes with Jane,
It doesn't mean that Jane's "just, plain."

Unwrap

Leaves fall in the darkness;
Wind still blows in the night.
Fear is honed in the quiet
When all is not in sight.

A Friend becomes a stranger;
Shadows wave in the wind;
Whistles become whispers;
A will begins to bend.

A song becomes a prayer;
A hum turns into screams;
The terror of the nighttime
Becomes a nightmare's dream.

The lasting night goes on
Black, packed tight in sweat;
On and on the night keeps on
A path with no regret.

You must move past the slight of hand
And recognize the lie.
The dark is there to terrify
Confuse and mystify.

The nighttime has no substance.
It's the things it hides behind.
Illuminate the hidden truth
And truth's not hard to find.

Names

"Why would your parents stick you with that?

Some names have pizzaz, and trill from the tongue,
But yours seems to clunk like a bell that's mis-rung.

Can't think of a name that sounds quite so silly.
You say it out loud and it flies willy-nilly.

Some people smirk when they hear your name said;
Others guffaw, while some hide their head.

It's sloppy at best and at worst it's just sleazy;
And defending your name must make you quite queasy.

So answer me please, if you have an idea,
Why your parents stuck you with—Onomatopoeia?"

"My answer to you, it's not what you think.
Oh sure at the start I did make a stink.

But Onomatopoeia's a name that just soars;
Or some days it's loud, on those days it roars.

I dip or I flip, as I dance through the air;
I swoop or I roll and I don't leave my chair.

Splat, rat-a-tat, meow, slip and slog;
My cat spilled the milk and got chased by the dog.

Whoop, I'm a crane. Honk, I'm a goose.
Squishing my hooves through the mud, I'm a moose.

My friends that I've made, they all understood.
My name made me strong and to them that was good.

You are who you are whatever you're named,
And a name's not a reason for being ashamed."

Fenway Forever

She was tall,
Blond, and stood out from
The kids hanging on the rail.
"Her father," she said, "used to sneak in."
She spoke about, "the hole near the left field stands."
Long gone;
"He sat," she said,"in the center field bleachers.
He saw a lot of 'Pesky's pole' homers.
He was there when the first 'K' was hung for Strikes.
He saw 'The Kid' hit home runs.
And saw Piersall run the bases backwards for his hundredth.
He moved to Michigan in the seventies,
Needing a job for his family;
Then listened on the night-time radio waves or
    occasionally TV,
As an errant fastball kept Tony C from the Hall of Fame,
And as 'The Rocket' flew and fell,
Fisk coaxed his home run, Buckner bobbled, but not
    in Fenway,
And through all those,"
The lady lowered her voice when she said, "In his words,
    'Damn Yankees'."
Kids cracked up.
Batting practice ended with
Ortiz crushing a towering homer to right.
The kids turned away from the diamond in the field to
    go to their seats.

The lady took out a white envelope,
Opened it carefully and deposited
The grainy, sandy contents over the rail and onto the field.
She turned and told her departing audience,
"He never saw the Sox win a World Series.
But as of this year, 2004, my Dad will never miss
    another chance."

The Incisor Man
(The Dentist)
(Inspired by Dr. Annicelle)

A bright white coat
A light blue mask,
The Incisor Man
Is right on the task.
Sharp as a pick,
The master of drill,
An unruly tooth
He's ready to fill.
Or a porcelain cap
To a tooth with a crack
And fixing a gap
With glue and a knack
For stuffing the gauze
And preparing the rinse
With only a pause
For a small recompense.
A flashy new toothbrush
Some toothpastes with mints
Some sagey advice
Always brush and then rinse.
Take care of your teeth,
Six months, get a check;
A bad tooth will be
More than pain in the neck.
He works with the speed

And the skill of X-Men
A professional demeanor
That's gentle times ten.
From aligning your jaw,
To emergency call,
The Incisor Man
Is the best of them all.

Today's Poem
(Crastinus)

My yellow #2 pencil
Started the day with a
Sharp point, gripped right,
And a rubber eraser to
Cover my mistakes.

By the middle of the day though,
It was well rested.
Then, when a thought
Could not show promise,
It wasted the day and
The point of it wore down
And the grip of it
Became a cold hand,
And the eraser
By itself
Cannot
Erase
Today's
Missed opportunities...

Timeless

What if time was never there?
Would you care?
If you were late,
Would they let you skate?
Wait?
You couldn't be late
At any rate.
If time's not there
Are you not anywhere?
Without our time,
There might never be crime.
How sublime,
No time for crime.
Perhaps our time
We could name it rhyme.
Hmmm?
And all my rhyme
Might turn to crime.
That couldn't work
It's kind of a quirk;
Time is always there to lurk.
No matter the name,
It stays the same.
If there wasn't time,
They'd have to invent it;
And I think we'd be glad
That somebody sent it.

Melody in Harmony for the Sake of Melody

The other day we struck a match:
To burn the flag
To burn a book
To burn the tree of liberty
To burn away stability.

Then you struck a chord,
To stop the hurt, the pain,
The pummeling down of raining shame.
I understood and loved you for the stand you took.

But I fear a greater loss.
Melody keeps the piece
From falling apart.
We must strike to stop the child's pain;
We must strike to change the tale to truth;
We must strike injustice everywhere it lives.

But we must live life—together,
Where damage control is a voice to reason,
And not the reason to walk away.

I hope our Melody will remain,
And we will strike to bring harmony again.
We are, in fact,
Much-Better-Together.

The Dream

The dream
Is to keep going,
Never to slow down,
Only to rest to contemplate:
The next adventure
And to never be bored;
Life should be like
A child views snowfall:
A wondrous gift,
A mixture of bright and pure,
Tempered with shimmering cold.
Too, the dream is learning
The greatness of happy and sad,
While adding enough spice and saltiness
Necessary to understand what I can.

Section 5

Santa's

A Christmas Story

If you've ever seen a boy or a girl
Too excited on Christmas Eve,
Then do what this Daddy decided to do
And they'll soon be asleep I believe.

Daddy had asked if his daughter had seen
A Gsnizzlerat under her bed,
And lifting the ruffle a little to see
She'd frowned and shaken her head.

"Oh Daddy, what is a Snizzlerat?"
Saying it tickled her nose,
She giggled a little in spite of herself
As she wiggled on out of her clothes.

"Now put on your nightgown and jump into bed
And I'll tell you a story that's true,
How a Gsnizzlerat came to live in a home
With a Dad and a girl just like you."

She settled in snuggly as warm as a bug
And her Daddy as part of his plan,
Gave her a kiss, she returned with a hug
And after awhile he began:

Once upon a time you know
And no one was to blame,
A fuzzy little animal
Was born without a name.

No other creature looked like him
With whiskers two feet long,
A droopy tail, and greeny scales,
And feet that just looked wrong.

People came and stared at him;
They mocked he's like no other.
They teased, in fact, he had a face
That's loved by just his mother.

Then Stuffy Oswald waddled in
With cane and stately coat,
And looking down he gave a frown
"Har-r-um-mphed" to clear his throat.

"It seems to me," was his decree,
"It's neither dog nor cat.
The only name that suits this shame
Is a name like Snizzlerat."

And then it stuck this long, odd name;
Its burden weighed him down.
He dragged his name where'er he went
And always wore a frown.

So slow to go meant eating late
On scraps or just a bone,
But what he learned to hate the most
Was eating all alone.

And then one day when months had passed
On Christmas Day it was
That Santa came to visit,
As Santa often does.

It wasn't really Santa Claus,
But a man dressed in his suit
With pillow stuffing hanging out
And a tied on beard to boot.

He brought his daughter Cristy.
He thought she understood
That helping those that needed help
Would always do some good.

She wore a little elf suit
And handed presents out;
But getting presents was to her
What Christmas was about.

Snizzlerat was called on first;
But dragging his heavy name,
It took so long, the gifts were gone;
The sack just left to claim.

He stared at Cristy's daddy;
And tears welled in his eyes.
In and out he heaved his chest
And made some awful cries.

Cristy thought... and thought some more
For something she could share.
Poor Snizzlerat was so, so sad,
His life seemed so unfair.

She knew she had to find a way
To help him understand
That beauty is inside of you
And she'd give him a hand.

Her Dad had given her a pin
At Christmas year before..
It was a G for her last name
And one she did adore.

Right then, she found the answer,
She took her golden G,
And pinned his name across his chest
For everyone to see.

Gsnizzlerat beamed from ear to ear.
He'd not forget this night.
He stood so tall the very next day
He'd grown a foot in height.

Because of Cristy's gesture
His name's not dragged through dirt.
He wears it pinned quite proudly
On the front of his t-shirt.

He kept up with the other kids
Then became the one who leads
Because he learned to love himself
He helps others with their needs.

The G is never spoken
Like love comes from the heart
And Cristy was amazed at what
A little love can start.

Christmas Day that evening,
Gsnizzlerat came to live
With Cristy and her Daddy
As they all had love to give.

His little girl listened right up to the end
And was trying with all of her might
But the last words she heard before falling asleep
Was her Daddy just saying, "Good night."

Santa's More Than Christmas

Somehow, Santa's more than Christmas
Somehow, more than mistletoe.
Somehow, seeds of Santa,
Somehow, seem to grow.

Somehow, peace is peaceful.
Somehow, silence goes with snow.
Somehow, songs sound like a symphony,
Somehow, everywhere you go.

Somehow, love spreads among the people;
Somehow, all around the world.
Somehow, Santa's more than Christmas;
Somehow, all the children know.

Somehow, Santa's Magic happens;
Somehow, presents under trees.
Somehow, smiles go best with giving.
Somehow, joy that Santa brings us, it never seems to leave.

Somehow, Santa's more than Christmas.
Somehow, if I may,
Somehow, I'm wishing Santa
Stays with us everyday.

Santa Lives

It is my supposition
That Santa's spirit lives
Through every generation,
Through a miracle that gives
To each and every person
With the goodness to respond,
To children being children
And their love to which we bond.

Each year, you can meet Santa
In the face of every child,
Whose giggles bring on sunshine
And twinkles, when they've smiled.
Through Nicholas in Myra
To Irving, and Dickens too,
Then Thomas Nast and Clement Moore
Through time each Santa flew.

Santa's many colors
Depends on every home,
'Cause Santa lives in more than Christmas,
No matter where you roam.

Though Santa keeps evolving
There's always been one aim,
That's helping "children who've been good"
To always be the same.

Acknowledgments

Without the help, support and encouragement of my wife Peg, my daughters Cristy and Kate, and my son-in-law, Paul; I never would have completed this book. The technical support and gentle nagging over the years, as well as their belief in the literary value of these poems, has made the difference.

Six years ago I became a member of a poetry group called The Faxon Poets. Over those years I received the benefit of critiques that always started with something positive, often followed by helpful suggestions for improvement. The critique format and being told that we should acknowledge ourselves as poets, made a very conducive literary haven for writing poetry. I cannot express how much that ambient climate has meant to me as well as the encouragement given by many members to complete this book.

About the Author

George Gould has been a writer most of his adult life. Mr. Gould states that his key to writing poetry was developed during his varied and diverse life experiences. From a young age he spent two summers hitchhiking and working across much of the United States. After achieving a BA in English, Mr. Gould held a wide variety of jobs that included banking, teaching, labor organizing, and contracts negotiations. He worked also as a deputy sheriff in corrections as well as helping to build nuclear turbines.

He began writing poetry in earnest after retiring, but many poems in this current book are poems well edited from when he wrote poems for his children and grandchildren.

George and his wife have resided in Connecticut for over forty years where they have developed an avid interest in birding and preservation of the environment.

George wants you to know that writing this book started as a labor of love and became another amazing life experience.

www.GeorgeGouldAuthor.com

www.ingramcontent.com/pod-product-compliance
Lightning Source LLC
Chambersburg PA
CBHW071231090426
42736CB00014B/3035